NATIONAL GEOGRAPHIC

READING EXPEDITION

PLANET PATROL

Wetland Adventure

By Rebecca L. Johnson

Illustrated by Matthew Archambault

PICTURE CREDITS
4 (top) © Tom Newsom; 6 (top to bottom)
© Karin Duthie/Alamy, © Wolfgang
Kaehler/Corbis; 7 Mapping Specialists, Ltd.;
64 © Michael Nichols/NGS Image Collection.

Produced through the worldwide resources of
the National Geographic Society, John M. Fahey,
Jr., President and Chief Executive Officer;
Gilbert M. Grosvenor, Chairman of the Board;
Nina D. Hoffman, Executive Vice President and
President, Books and Education Publishing
Group.

**PREPARED BY NATIONAL GEOGRAPHIC
SCHOOL PUBLISHING**
Ericka Markman, Senior Vice President and
President, Children's Books and Education
Publishing Group; Steve Mico, Senior Vice
President, Publisher, Editorial Director; Francis
Downey, Executive Editor; Richard Easby,
Editorial Manager; Bea Jackson, Director of
Design; Cynthia Olson, Art Director; Margaret
Sidlosky, Director of Illustrations; Matt
Wascavage, Manager of Publishing Services;
Lisa Pergolizzi, Sean Philpotts, Production
Managers, Ted Tucker, Production Specialist.

MANUFACTURING AND QUALITY CONTROL
Christopher A. Liedel, Chief Financial Officer;
Phillip L. Schlosser, Director; Clifton M. Brown,
Manager.

EDITORS
Barbara Seeber, Mary Anne Wengel

BOOK DEVELOPMENT
Morrison BookWorks LLC

BOOK DESIGN
Steven Curtis Design

ART DIRECTION
Dan Banks, Project Design Company

Published by the National Geographic Society
1145 17th Street, N.W.
Washington, D.C. 20036-4688

ISBN: 0-7922-5854-1

2010 2009 2008 2007 2006
1 2 3 4 5 6 7 8 9 10 11 12 13 14 15

Contents

African Adventure

Dr. Bender was e-mailing the four young people who had sent in the best applications to the advertisement he'd posted a month before. He finished typing the message. Then he added the four e-mail addresses. He clicked the send button. Nate, Jessie, Rashel, and Mick were about to learn they'd soon be off on an African adventure!

Nate Carter, age 13
Vista, California
I've always wanted to visit Africa, ever since I saw my first elephant at the San Diego Zoo. I'm a volunteer there now!

Rashel de Marco, age 11
Belle Glade, Florida
I live just north of the Everglades, the largest wetland in the United States. I'd like to explore Okavango and see how the two wetlands compare.

Attention Young Explorers!

Would you like to study one of Africa's rarest birds in one of the world's largest wetlands? EcoAware is dedicated to promoting science and environmental awareness around the world. We want to involve young people in our research projects. EcoAware will give four students, ages 11 to 13, a chance to work with Dr. Neville Makutsi in Botswana, Africa, for one month. Dr. Makutsi studies wattled cranes nesting in the Okavango River Delta in northwestern Botswana. If you are interested, fill out the application. Send it to Dr. Alan Bender at EcoAware.

Mick Roubideaux, age 12
Alliance, Nebraska
Cranes are my favorite birds. Every year, sandhill cranes migrate through Nebraska on their way to Canada to breed.

Jessie Mendez, age 13
Alma, New Mexico
I live on a cattle ranch and love being outside. I want to be a scientist who studies animals when I grow up.

Botswana

After the interns accepted their assignment, Dr. Bender e-mailed this fact sheet about Botswana to them.

Botswana

Botswana is a country on the continent of Africa. Most of the country is covered by desert. But in its northwestern corner is a huge wetland called the Okavango Delta. How did this wetland form? It formed with the help of a river.

The Okavango River doesn't empty into another body of water like most rivers. Instead, it flows into a swamp in the desert. This swamp is called the Okavango Delta. The delta is a wild wetland.

The Okavango Delta attracts many large animals. The animals come to drink water and eat the plants that grow here. The delta is home to over 400 kinds of birds. One of these is the wattled crane. It is among Africa's rarest birds. Only about 8,000 are left in the wild.

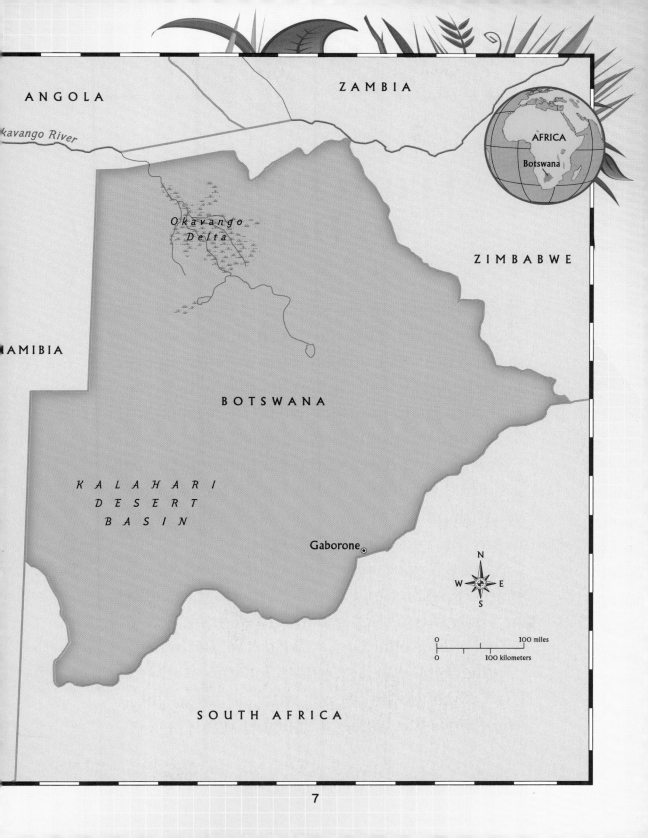

ANGOLA

ZAMBIA

kavango River

AFRICA

Botswana

Okavango
Delta

ZIMBABWE

NAMIBIA

BOTSWANA

KALAHARI
DESERT
BASIN

Gaborone ⊛

N
W ⊕ E
S

0   100 miles
0   100 kilometers

SOUTH AFRICA

CHAPTER 1

From Desert to Delta

Jessie stared out the window of the plane. Only a few trees dotted the desert landscape below. She and the other three interns were flying over the Kalahari Desert. Dr. Bender was with them. In about 15 minutes, they would be landing in Gaborone, the capital city of Botswana.

She glanced down at the book in her lap. "Hey, listen to this," Jessie said, nudging Rashel who was sitting next to her. "The word *Kalahari* means 'the great thirst,'" she read.

"That's a good way to describe a desert," replied Rashel. She paused. "I guess that makes the Okavango Delta 'the great big drink.'"

Dr. Bender chuckled. "Good one, Rashel!"

Nate chimed in. "I've been looking at the map. The Okavango River ends with the delta. But where does the water in the delta go?"

"I know the answer to that one," said Mick excitedly. "I read that most of the water that enters the delta **evaporates.** What's left seeps into the ground."

Jessie turned to the window again. "Not many roads down there," she mused. "I wonder how we're getting to Okavango from Gaborone."

The "fasten seatbelts" sign lit up.

"You won't have long to wonder," replied Dr. Bender. "We'll be meeting Dr. Makutsi soon."

Ten minutes later, the plane taxied up to the terminal. The interns and Dr. Bender climbed down the stairs that had been rolled to the

----

evaporate − to change from a liquid to a gas

doorway of the plane. Overhead, the sun blazed. Shimmering heat waves rose from the runway. The air was hot and dry.

A tall African man with cropped hair stood waiting at the bottom of the stairs. He recognized Dr. Bender instantly.

"Alan!" he shouted, waving.

"Nev!" Dr. Bender called, striding over and grabbing the scientist's hand. "Kids, I'd like you all to meet Dr. Neville Makutsi. He's one of the best bird biologists in all of Africa."

Dr. Bender introduced the interns individually. They each shook Dr. Makutsi's hand. Dr. Makutsi smiled a huge grin that made the interns feel instantly at ease.

A voice on a loudspeaker mounted outside the terminal announced that another flight was boarding immediately.

Dr. Bender looked surprised. "Oh, no!" he said. "That's my flight. I thought we'd have more time to talk!" He pulled four books with dark green covers from his bag. They were stamped with the EcoAware logo.

"Here you go," he said, handing each intern a book. "These are your official journals. Write down everything you see and do and learn. You'll find them useful in writing up your final reports to EcoAware."

Dr. Bender looked at the interns. "I've got to run! Good luck at Okavango! I'll look forward to hearing all about your adventures when I come back next month." The interns waved goodbye.

"Dr. Makutsi," Nate began after Dr. Bender was gone, "how are we getting to Okavango?"

"Call me Nev," the scientist said kindly. But to answer your question, I'm going to fly us there," he said, pointing to a small plane parked just beyond the terminal. "It's a long way to Okavango. There are few good roads. It's easier to fly."

"Awesome!" Mick blurted out. "A scientist with his own plane!"

Nev laughed. "It's the university's," he said. "They just loan it to me when I'm working in the field."

The scientist helped the interns collect their bags. They headed for the small plane. They loaded their gear and climbed aboard.

Nev slid into the pilot's seat in the cockpit. He turned back to the interns who were squeezing into the narrow seats in the main compartment.

"One of you can sit beside me in the copilot's seat, if you'd like," Nev said.

Four hands shot up into the air. Nev chuckled. "OK, OK, let's start at the beginning of the alphabet. You'll be first, Jessie."

The others looked disappointed. "Don't worry," Nev smiled as he called back over his shoulder. "You'll all get a chance to be up front before the month is over. You might even get sick of flying!"

The interns looked at each other wide-eyed. They didn't believe they could ever get sick of flying.

Nev began flipping switches on the control panel. The engines whined. The propellers began to turn faster and faster. Then they were off! The plane taxied down the runway and soared up into the air.

"Nev," Jessie asked, talking loudly above the drone of the engines, "do people in Botswana speak Botswanan?"

"The official language is English," Nev replied, "but the native language we speak is called Setswana."

Jessie pulled out her journal. She cracked it open and began taking notes.

"You will learn many Setswana words while you are here," Nev said, looking back at the others. "But one of the most important is *pula.* It is the word for our currency, like *dollar* is the word for yours. But pula also means rain, and in a country as dry as ours, rain is life. Pula is such an important word that people often use it when they make a toast to celebrate something."

It was hard to talk above the noise of the engines. The interns fell silent, watching the world move past below. The landscape was dry and sandy with a few scattered trees. Every now and then they flew over a small village. In each village, the round houses were clustered together around a well.

Mick yawned and stretched. The endless desert was getting boring. He leaned over so he could see out of the cockpit window. Ahead in the distance, there was a dark patch on the horizon. "Nev! What's that up there?" he asked, pointing.

"That, my young friend," said Nev, "is the Okavango Delta!"

Twenty minutes later, the vast delta spread out below them. Flat and green, it stretched for miles. It was a mixture of grassy swamps and shallow lagoons. Narrow **channels** linked one lagoon to the next. They cut watery pathways through huge patches of reeds and grass.

"The rains in Angola were heavy this year," Nev said. "The amount of water in the delta has been rising for the past few months." He began explaining how the delta changed during the year as water levels rose and fell.

"You are here at the best time—the middle of the dry season," Nev said, angling the plane downward. "Most of the country is dry and brown. But the Okavango Delta is full of water. It is like an oasis. It is bursting with life."

channel − a body of water that connects lagoons

15

The Okavango Delta

by Jessie

The Okavango Delta is fed by the Okavango River. The river begins 800 miles to the north, in the highlands of Angola. During the wet season in Angola, heavy rains fall. The water runs into the Okavango River. This mass of floodwater travels south to Botswana. It reaches the delta in May and June. The delta gets bigger as the water arrives. Then, over the next few months, the water slowly evaporates. The delta gets smaller again. The following year, the arrival of the floodwaters starts the process all over again.

Rashel saw grayish-brown shapes moving through the grass down on the ground. She caught her breath as she realized what they were. "Look!" she cried. "Elephants!"

"Where? Where?" Nate cried, trying to see.

"Hang on," said Nev, banking the plane into a turn. The interns sat spellbound as Nev flew the plane in a big circle above the elephant herd.

After completing the turn, Nev angled the plane's nose down more sharply. The plane started to descend. The interns spotted other

animals as they got closer.
They saw a giraffe munching
leaves and a mother warthog
with four little ones. Straight
ahead they saw a herd of zebras.
Spooked by the noise of the
engines, the zebras took off at a
gallop. They kicked up their heels
as they ran.

"What a perfect place for animals,"
Mick said, watching the zebras run.

"Yes," Nev agreed. "Perfect for
elephants, zebras, and wattled cranes.
Okavango is an ideal nursery for cranes.
As you know, I'm studying nesting cranes in
this part of the delta. You'll be helping me find
nests and count chicks. We'll also be recording
what the chicks eat and how fast they grow."

The plane soared over a cluster of tall trees.
Farther ahead, several tan-colored tents were
staked out in the middle of a big grassy area.

"That's the camp," Nev said, pointing. "It will
be our home for the next month." He checked the
controls. "Better tighten your seatbelts," he
announced. "We're about to land."

"But where's the runway?" Nate asked, as he scanned the ground below.

"Runway?" Nev said with a laugh. "There isn't one. Hang on!"

The plane swooped down. For a few seconds, it skimmed along just above the grass. Then the wheels touched down. *Bump, bump, bump.* Nev brought the plane to a stop a few hundred yards from the tents.

He shut off the engines. The propellers slowed and stopped spinning. Nev slid out of his seat and walked back through the plane. He opened the side door and jumped down. Then he helped the interns climb out.

For a moment Nev and the interns just stood in the warm sun. They stretched and breathed in the scents of Okavango—the grass and water and wild animals. Then they picked up their gear and started toward the camp.

At that moment, a lion came out from behind one of the tents.

Water World

The interns stopped dead in their tracks. Rashel felt her mouth go dry. Her heart was pounding. She wanted to run, but her legs refused to move.

"SHOO!" Nev suddenly shouted at the lion, waving his arm.

The lion took a step back. It looked at Nev and then it turned and ran.

The interns watched the lion loping through the grass. It disappeared into some tall bushes far beyond the camp.

Jessie raised an eyebrow and looked at Nev. "'Shoo'? All you have to do to scare away a lion is say 'shoo'?"

Nev shook his head, laughing. "It only works with this lion. He is very young and very shy. He only comes around when no one is home."

"Will other lions, who are less shy, be coming into our camp?" asked Rashel in a nervous voice.

"Not likely," replied Nev. "But Okavango is a wild place. You never know."

Rashel swallowed hard.

Nev showed the interns around. There were four big tents. One was for the boys, and one was for the girls. Their beds were low wooden cots. Nev had his own tent. The fourth tent was both the kitchen and the office.

After the interns had unpacked their things, they followed Nev into the kitchen tent.

"You've had a long trip," Nev said, "and a little excitement!" He winked at Rashel. "So how about something to eat?"

"Great! I'm starving!" said Mick, pulling up a camp chair. Nodding in agreement, the others sat down around the long folding table. Nev passed out plates, cups, and silverware.

"I thought you'd enjoy having a traditional Botswana meal," Nev said. "How does roasted goat, **sorghum,** and corn porridge sound?" He studied the interns with a twinkle in his eye. "And mopane caterpillars for dessert?"

No one spoke. Nev burst out laughing. He set a big platter of sandwiches and fruit in the middle of the table. The interns heaved a sigh of relief and helped themselves to the meal.

"I would like you to try the traditional food while you're here," Nev added.

"That sounds good," replied Rashel. "I may pass on the caterpillars, though."

Eating caterpillars.
by Nate
Nev told us that the leaves of the mopane tree are very nutritious. They are eaten by the caterpillars of the Emperor moth. The moth lays its eggs on the leaves. After the eggs hatch, the green-and-blue spiky caterpillars eat the leaves. Local people eat the caterpillars!

sorghum – an edible tropical grass

After lunch, Nev gave each intern binoculars and a canteen of water. The interns all had their journals, too.

"We have to purify the water before we can drink it," said Nev, showing them the big container in which the water was stored. "Always take water with you when we go out into the field. You can get pretty thirsty when it's hot," Nev said. "Now, let's explore the Okavango Delta."

They set out, heading toward what looked like a green meadow in the distance. Surprisingly, the grass they were walking through was brown and dry. It made a soft *shush-shush* sound as they walked.

"Remember, it is the dry season," Nev said. "The grasses are green near the water, but away from it, they are quite dry right now. Even though we are in a wetland, grass fires are common in Okavango this time of year."

A fishing eagle soared overhead. Then two impala ran past. They were just a blur of tawny coats and long, curved horns.

Nev and the interns walked past several termite mounds. A big lizard was basking in the

sun on top of one. At the base of another, several young baboons were playing.

The grass began getting greener and taller. Nev took the lead, pushing through reeds that grew as high as his waist. Rashel was just about to ask about snakes when the reeds gave way to water. They were standing on the edge of a narrow channel.

"Give me a hand, will you?" Nev asked the interns. They hadn't noticed the long wooden boat stashed in the reeds. They helped Nev slide it into the water.

"Climb in, everyone," Nev said. "This boat is called a *mokoro*. It is a good way to get around in the delta."

The interns sat single file in the bottom of the mokoro. Nev stood up in the back. With a long pole he pushed off against the bank. The mokoro went gliding out into the channel.

Nev slowly poled the mokoro along. The water was still and cool. A school of fish darted past. Huge water lilies floated on the surface of the water. The interns watched as a bird with incredibly long legs and toes stepped from lily pad to lily pad.

Water Means Life   by Rashel
In the wetland, whatever the water touches is green and growing. There are so many different kinds of plants along the waterways that I couldn't begin to list them all. Lots of insects hatch in the water, too. The plants and the insects are food for all sorts of animals, from huge elephants to tiny swallows.

Nev pointed out a kind of antelope called a red lechwe wading in the water ahead. A little later they saw a bushbuck, a sitatunga, and several Cape buffalo. Nev told them the name of each animal in Setswana. He also told them the names of some animals they hadn't seen yet.

Suddenly, snorting sounds came from farther along the waterway. Nev jammed the pole into the muddy bottom of the channel. The mokoro stopped moving.

"What's making those snorting noises?" Jessie whispered to Nev.

"Hippos," Nev replied softly. "See there? They have just surfaced."

Three massive heads rose out of the water. One of the hippos opened its mouth wide.

Very slowly, Nev guided the mokoro over to the shore. "Hippos are some of the most

List of animals (English/Setswana)   by Nate
fish — tlhapi
frog — segwagwa
ant – tshoswane
bird – nonyane
baboon — tshwene
beetle – khukhwane
hippo — kubu
leopard — nkwe
lion — tau
elephant — tlou
snake — noga

tlhapi

segwagwa

dangerous animals in Africa," he whispered. "They don't like to be disturbed. They can move very fast both in and out of the water."

The mokoro slid into the reeds and up onto the bank. "We'll walk the rest of the way," Nev said quietly, helping the interns out of the boat.

They followed Nev through the reeds and up onto drier ground. When they reached a termite mound, he stopped and crouched down. He held his finger to his lips when he turned to look at them.

"My young friends," he said quietly, pulling out his binoculars, "I'd like to introduce you to your first wattled cranes." All four interns turned their binoculars to where Nev was pointing.

"Wow!" said Mick softly. "They're beautiful!"

"I didn't think they'd be so big!" Jessie added.

Fifty feet away, two wattled cranes were standing beside their nest of dry grass. Inside the nest was a chick. The cranes were mostly white, but their backs were ashy gray. The edges of their wings were black. Their long legs and feet were black, too.

Hanging down just under the cranes' beaks were two fleshy flaps—their wattles. It was these strange features that gave the birds their name.

The adults never left the chick alone. One of them stood guard while the other poked its beak into the soft ground, searching for tender roots. It fed the chick very gently, putting the food right into its mouth.

"Wattled cranes nest only in wetlands," Nev explained. "Based on the last crane survey, there

are about 1,200 cranes in the Okavango. That's more wattled cranes in one spot than any other place in Africa. About 250 of those 1,200 cranes are breeding pairs. So there are about 120 or so nests."

"Are we going to survey each one of those nests?" Jessie asked.

Nev shook his head. "We have about 30 nests to monitor. Other biologists are doing the rest."

The sun was getting low in the sky. "Time to go," Nev said, putting away his binoculars. "But don't worry. We'll return first thing tomorrow."

Back at camp, Nev made a stew with rice for dinner. They each ate two big bowls of it. Then Nev walked them to their tents. It had quickly gotten dark. The night sky was full of stars. Nate had never seen so many stars in his life.

Amazing Cranes   by Mick

Today we saw our first wattled cranes. The adults stand 5 feet tall! Nev said they weigh about 14 pounds. It's almost impossible to tell if an adult crane is male or female. They're almost identical. The chick looks like a huge duckling. It is covered with fluffy down. It has a big head, long legs, and huge feet!

"Nev," Rashel said a little nervously, pausing in front of her tent, "do you think the lion will come into camp while we're sleeping?"

"It's possible," he replied. "But most animals rarely bother people without a good reason. Stay inside your tent and you should be perfectly safe. If animals walk through the camp, it's usually because they are trying to get somewhere else."

Rashel nodded and said good night. But she wasn't sure she really believed the part about being safe.

CHAPTER 3

Nest Watch

Just after dawn, Rashel woke up with a start. She heard noises. There was something outside the tent.

"*Pssst!* Jessie!" she hissed. "Wake up!"

A grumbling moan came from Jessie's cot. "Go back to sleep!"

"No, I'm serious!" she whispered hoarsely. "There's some kind of animal outside!"

Jessie sat up, looking annoyed. She rolled out of her cot and padded over to the tent door in her bare feet. "Rashel, I'm telling you," she said throwing the tent flap back, "there is nothing—"

Jessie froze. She just stared. Behind her, Rashel stared too.

Not twenty feet away was an elephant— a really big elephant. It was walking behind another elephant. Behind it were two smaller elephants. Between them was an even smaller baby elephant.

The adult elephants were making very low rumbling noises. Their huge heads swayed slightly from side to side. They were walking slowly so the baby could keep up.

Rashel was terrified. What if the elephants came this way? What if they walked into the tent and crushed her and Jessie?

Then she noticed how gently and carefully the elephants were walking. They looked at Jessie and Rashel with their small, twinkling eyes. But they just kept going.

Nev was right. They were just animals with somewhere to go. They didn't mean any harm.

Jessie and Rashel didn't say a word until the elephants disappeared from view.

Then they turned as Nate let out a *whoop!* He was standing outside his tent in his pajamas. He was grinning from ear to ear.

"Wasn't that absolutely, positively the most FANTASTIC thing you've ever seen?" he said, holding his arms triumphantly over his head.

Beyond him, Nev stood in the doorway of the cooking tent. He was smiling, too.

Over breakfast, Nev went through the plan for the day. Half an hour later, they were on their way to the first wattled crane nest. In their daypacks were binoculars, lunch, sunscreen, insect repellent, canteens of water, their journals, and two GPS, or global positioning system, units.

Nev had explained how to use GPS. "These are devices that use satellites orbiting Earth to pinpoint your exact location. We can use them to figure out precisely where each of the crane nests is located."

When they arrived at the first nest, Jessie turned on the GPS. It locked onto several satellites. A set of numbers appeared on the GPS's little screen. They were the exact latitude and longitude of their position. Jessie wrote the numbers down in her journal under the heading *Nest 1, Location.*

There was a single chick in Nest 1, just like the nest they'd visited the day before.

"That's normal," Nev explained, watching the chick through his binoculars. "Wattled cranes raise only one chick at a time. That's one reason why the crane population is so **vulnerable.** If something happens to their chick before it is old enough to survive on its own, the parents have to wait an entire year to have another chick."

Nest 1 was about 20 feet from the water. Every few minutes one of the crane parents walked down to the water's edge. When it came back, it carried something in its bill that it fed to the chick.

"What is the crane feeding the chick?" Rashel asked Nev.

"Water lily roots," he replied. "Cranes eat tender roots and plant shoots. They also eat insects. You need to learn to recognize what the chicks are eating so you can record it."

Suddenly, a shadow flickered across the nest. Nate glanced up to see a fishing eagle that was circling overhead. Instinctively, the chick ducked

---

vulnerable - open to attack or damage, easily wounded

down in the nest to hide. Both of the parents threw back their heads and called loudly. The eagle flew away.

"That's a guard call," Nev explained. "It's used to scare something away. It also warns the chick that danger is near."

Jessie wrote down some information and made a little sketch in her journal of how the crane looked when it made the guard call. Then she made a few other sketches of crane behaviors they'd observed.

The Wattled Crane   by Jessie

Unlike most birds, wattled cranes raise only one chick in a nesting season. They sometimes lay two eggs. But as soon as the first egg hatches, the parents stop incubating the other egg. That sounds cruel. But Nev said if two chicks hatched at the same time, they'd fight to the death. Wow! Bird biologists think the second egg is laid as insurance—just in case the first one doesn't hatch or gets destroyed.

Guard Call

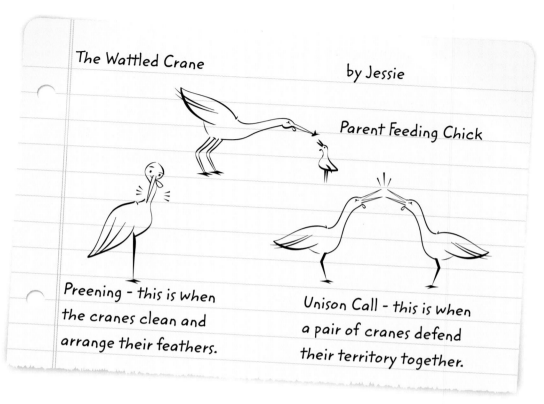

The Wattled Crane   by Jessie

Parent Feeding Chick

Preening - this is when the cranes clean and arrange their feathers.

Unison Call - this is when a pair of cranes defend their territory together.

After watching the nest for a few more minutes, the team moved on to the next nest. It was about 500 yards away. The parent cranes at Nest 2 were feeding their chick green bugs.

Nest 3 was right at the edge of a waterway. Just as they were about to start making observations, they heard loud splashing sounds. A big hippo came charging out from the reeds. Water streamed off its pinkish-brown body.

The hippo kept running. The crane's nest, and the chick, were directly in its path!

The parent cranes called frantically. They flapped their wings. They hopped up and down. But the chick seemed frozen with fear. The interns watched in horror as the hippo closed in on the nest. Rashel shut her eyes, sure the chick was going to be squashed.

But at the last moment, the hippo swerved. It narrowly missed the nest. It kept on running until it disappeared into another clump of reeds some distance away.

Mick let out a huge sigh. "That was close!"

By noon, Nev and the interns had surveyed five nests. Nev's plan was that each day, they would check out 10 of the 30 nests in his study area. That meant they would survey all 30 nests every three days.

Nests 6 through 11 were on an island in a lagoon. The team had to take the mokoro to get there. They ate their lunch in the boat, watching a pair of bushbucks nibble on young plants. After lunch, they walked to Nest 6.

Nate focused his binoculars on the nest while the others were still settling in. Two adult cranes were feeding in the brown grass near the nest. He frowned.

"Nev, I don't see a chick," he whispered.

Nev and the others watched the pair of cranes for several minutes. Finally, Nev spoke. "I don't think this chick survived. The parents are not behaving like they have a chick to care for."

"What happened to it?" Jessie asked.

"We'll never know for sure," Nev replied. "Perhaps it was eaten by a snake or an eagle. Perhaps it was sick and died."

"That's sad," Rashel said softly.

"In a way, yes," Nev responded. "But it is how things work in nature. Some chicks don't make it. But we hope that enough chicks will survive to keep the total population of cranes the same from year to year."

The interns finished taking notes about Nest 6. Just as they were about to leave, they heard the sound of a plane.

"There it is!" cried Mick, pointing just above the horizon.

The plane was flying low. As it passed directly overhead, the interns smiled and waved.

But Nev didn't wave. He was studying the plane through his binoculars. It was turning, starting to circle back.

"Who do you suppose it is, Nev?" Mick asked. "Other scientists? Maybe tourists?"

Nev sounded angry when he replied. "No. I recognize the plane. It belongs to a company that builds water pipelines."

"Why are they flying over Okavango?" Mick asked. "Are there pipelines in the delta?"

Nev sighed. "No, we've kept them out so far. Water is valuable in this part of the world. Many people need it and want it. Several years ago,

some politicians proposed building canals and pipelines that would carry water from the delta to cities and industries."

"What happened?" Rashel asked.

"Many people protested," Nev answered. "They pointed out that canals and pipelines could carry away too much water. Anything that changes the amount of water in the delta will **impact** the plants. And what changes the plants will affect the animals, including wattled cranes."

The plane had completed its turn. It was going to pass over them again.

The scientist sighed deeply. "Right now there are only about 8,000 wattled cranes left in Africa. A good number of those live and nest here. If the Okavango loses too much water, the habitat for these rare birds may be lost. The Okavango is critical for their survival."

"What's happening with the pipeline idea now?" Nate asked.

Nev frowned. "Luckily, the original plans to build the pipeline were set aside. But the threat has not passed. If there is a serious drought, some

---

impact − to affect the outcome of something

people will likely want to take water out of Okavango again."

"Are some of those people in the plane?" Rashel asked, looking up.

"I would guess so," Nev replied softly.

Jessie had been quiet for some time. "Boy, the cranes here sure do face a lot of dangers," she said. "Their chicks get eaten by snakes and other predators. They risk getting stomped by hippos. And there's a chance that people could take the water and destroy their **habitat.**"

"And that last danger is the biggest one," Nev said. "That's because it can harm all the cranes in the delta and a lot of other animals, too."

They heard the sound of the plane's engine again. The interns looked up as the plane flew overhead. This time they didn't wave.

---

habitat – a place where a plant or animal naturally lives and grows

Smoke in the Sky

A week had passed since the interns and Nev had spotted the pipeline company's plane. They had fallen into a daily routine. They got up at sunrise. By 8 a.m. they were out in the field surveying nests. They finished around 6 p.m. and headed back to camp. Then they ate dinner. By the time it got dark, they were ready for bed.

"We're getting to be like a lot of the animals in Okavango," Mick observed. "We get up when the sun rises. And we go to bed when it sets."

When they got up, they often found signs that animals had been in camp during the night. Once they found leopard tracks! Another time they discovered that a baboon had gotten into the kitchen tent. It had eaten all of their bananas.

The Nighttime Thief   by Rashel
Last night there was a thief in camp! Someone didn't zip up the flap securely on the kitchen tent before we went to bed. No one heard anything. But in the morning we discovered banana peels everywhere! Nev guessed it was a baboon.

Every morning at breakfast, the interns sat at the computer with Nev. They put together all the information they'd collected the day before. With the GPS readings, they'd made a map of the study area. Each one of the 30 nests was marked with a red dot on the map.

For each nest, they had also created a data page. There they recorded information about what the cranes were feeding their chicks. They also described how quickly the chicks were growing and what new things they were learning to do. Every third day they took the plane and flew around the study area for an hour. They got a bird's-eye view of all the nests from the air.

Jessie was sitting at the table, reviewing the data pages. "Today we go back to Area 2, Nests 11 through 20."

"Good. That's my favorite part," Nate said as he poured milk on his cereal. It was powdered milk mixed with water. At first he'd thought it tasted funny. But he was starting to like it.

"Why do you like Area 2?" Rashel asked, slicing a mango.

"First, because it's close to camp, so we don't have to walk so far," Nate replied. "And second, because it's got that huge termite mound."

After breakfast they gathered up their gear and headed off to Area 2. The chick in Nest 11 was sleeping. Everyone could see the parents, which were feeding close to the nest.

At Nest 12, the chick was following its parents as they walked through the grass. When they stuck their bills into the soft soil in search of insects, so did the chick.

"They learn by doing," Nev commented. "And they grow so fast. Notice how much bigger the chicks are in just a week? At the end of three months, that chick will be as tall as its parents. At the end of four months, it will be able to fly."

"How long before young cranes raise chicks of their own?" Nate asked.

"Not until they are four to eight years old," Nev replied. "We think wattled cranes live an average of about 20 to 30 years. Some may live much longer."

Data for Nest 12   by Mick
Nest description: large nest built entirely of grass; roughly 20 feet from the edge of a waterway

Chick notes: single chick; seemed smaller than other chicks at first; now growing rapidly; has begun following parents as they look for food; feathers have replaced fluffy down

The scientist put away his binoculars. "When everyone is ready, let's move on to Nest 13."

Nate swung his pack onto his back. "Nev, I'm ready now. Do you mind if I go on ahead? Between here and Nest 13 is that huge termite mound I like to climb. Who knows, today I might get to see the elephant herd."

Nev nodded, smiling. "No problem, Nate. We'll catch up."

Nate hurried off, running through the grass.

Twenty minutes later, Nev and the other interns spotted Nate sitting on top of the termite mound. He was looking off into the distance.

"See any elephants, Nate?" Rashel called out as they walked up.

"No," Nate said slowly. "No elephants. But I think I see smoke."

Nev frowned and set down his pack. Then he stepped up to where Nate was sitting. Through his binoculars, Nev saw a band of dark smoke quickly stretching along the horizon. The fire was only about a mile away.

"It's a grass fire," Nev explained when he and Nate were back on the ground. He glanced in the direction of the fire. "The wind is behind it, so the fire is coming this way."

"Right toward these nests?" Jessie asked.

Nev nodded. "Yes. And that's a problem. The chicks can't fly, so they can't escape a fire."

Nev dug through his backpack. He pulled out their map of the study zone that showed the locations of all the nests. He spread it out on the ground. The interns gathered around.

"If the fire keeps coming this way, it will reach the nesting area right here," Nev said, pointing to a spot on the map. "It will hit Nests 13, 14, and 15 first. Then it will probably move through the rest of Area 2."

Nev looked at the interns gathered around him. His face was very serious. "If the fire reaches Area 2, all the chicks here could die."

Mick's mind was racing. "Could we go up in the plane and drop water on the fire?"

"That's a good idea, Mick," said Nev. "But we'd need a lot of water. And I don't have any big containers. Just a few buckets at camp."

Jessie had been studying the map. "What we need is a firebreak."

Rashel frowned. "What's that?"

"You dig up the ground to create a strip of dirt between you and a fire," she explained. "The dirt can't burn, so the fire stops."

"Do you know how to make one?" Nate asked.

Jessie nodded. "On the ranch where I live in New Mexico, wildfires are a big problem. They are really bad when it's dry, like it is here. I've helped my parents make firebreaks before, when fires were coming toward the house. We always got the fire to stop."

She looked at Nev. "How many shovels do you have at camp?"

"Just two," he replied.

"That may be enough," Jesse said.

"We can take turns," Nate said. "Two can dig. The other three can throw water on the grass along the firebreak. That will help, too."

"It's worth a try," Rashel urged.

Nev nodded and stood up. "The cranes face so many dangers that we can't do anything about. But in this case, maybe we can help. Let's go!"

They sprinted back to camp. Nev and Nate got the shovels while Mick grabbed three metal buckets. Jessie and Rashel filled all the canteens with drinking water.

By the time they were back at the termite mound, the fire was much closer.

When they reached Nest 13, the parent cranes were walking back and forth. They kept looking in the direction of the fire, fluffing their wings.

"They know something is wrong," Nev said, as they hurried past.

Fifty yards beyond the nest, Jessie stopped. She glanced at the map.

"We should dig the fire break here," she said.

Nev dug into the ground with a shovel. He turned over a big clump of dirt. "The ground is soft. It's not too bad." He and Mick worked side by side. They dug as fast as they could.

Jessie grabbed the buckets and handed them to Rashel and Nate.

"Let's get water," she said, heading for the reeds. "We'll soak the grass on either side of the fire break."

They worked steadily. Every few minutes they switched places. Digging was a hard job.

After a while, Jessie stood back. The firebreak was about thirty feet long. They were making progress. But it wasn't nearly long enough.

"Keep digging!" she cried.

They could smell the smoke now, strong and sharp. Behind them, the cranes in Nest 13 flapped their wings nervously. They kept touching their chick with their long bills. The chick extended its body and made loud distress calls.

The smoke grew thicker and thicker. Nev and the interns watched it roll in like a dark gray fog. It swirled around them, making them choke and cough. Nev stared in the direction of the fire. For a moment the smoke parted. He saw orange flames leaping across the ground.

"We're out of time!" he cried. "The fire is almost here. Everyone stop shoveling and move away from the fire and smoke!"

The interns moved back. They saw the flames, too. And now they could hear the fire as well. It crackled and snapped.

"Be ready to run to the water," shouted Nev, pulling the interns farther back from the break. "If the flames look like they are going to cross over to this side, we have to get out of here!"

The interns nodded. They stood silently and watched the fire. It was moving toward them like an angry animal on the run.

The Rescuers' Tale

The flames leaped along in front of the wind. They jumped from one clump of grass to the next.

The fire was 20 feet from the firebreak. Then 10 feet. Then 5 feet. The smoke was so thick it was hard to breathe. Behind Nev and the interns, the cranes were squawking loudly.

The fire kept coming. They could feel its heat on their faces.

The flames reached the far edge of the firebreak. Tongues of flames shot out onto the damp soil. They sizzled and died.

A gust of wind fanned the fire. A single flame arched across the break. The grass on the other side started to smolder.

Jessie turned, ready to run. Then she realized she was still holding a bucket. It was nearly full of water. She swung the bucket forward. Her aim was perfect. The water streamed out and doused the growing flame.

Breathlessly, they watched and waited. The flames beyond the firebreak began to die down. They flickered lower and lower. Then they went out. The fire had run out of grass to burn.

"It worked!" Nate shouted. "We did it!"

They stared out at the blackened landscape. In some places it was still smoking. But the fire was over. They had saved the cranes.

They picked up the shovels and the buckets. Then they started walking back toward the camp. Everyone was streaked with dirt and sweat.

They were close enough to see the tents when they heard the sound of an engine. Up in the sky, a plane was circling. It began to descend. "I think they're going to land," Mick said.

Suddenly he recognized the plane. They all did. It was the plane they had seen earlier that was owned by the pipeline company.

The plane landed gently in the grass. It taxied slowly to a stop. The door in the side opened. The pilot jumped out. She was wearing a dark blue flight suit with a logo on the chest.

Stepping out behind her were two men. They wore expensive suits. One was tall with dark hair. The other was short with blonde hair.

The last person out of the plane was a man wearing a tan vest with many pockets. He had three cameras hanging around his neck.

The pilot walked up to Nev and the interns. She took off her sunglasses.

"Lily Tomasutke," she said, shaking Nev's hand politely. "We saw the fire from the air. I knew your camp was close. I wanted to make sure everyone was all right."

"We're fine," Nev replied, "tired and very dirty, but fine."

"We dug a firebreak," Rashel explained. "We stopped the fire before it reached the cranes."

"What cranes are those?" Lily asked, smiling.

"Wattled cranes," Nate spoke up. "One of the most endangered birds in all of Africa."

The tall man cleared his throat loudly. "Everyone here seems to be fine," he said curtly. "Let's go."

Reluctantly, Lily started to say goodbye. "I'm sorry," she said. "He's my boss. I have to go."

But just then, the man with the cameras stepped forward.

"Hi! I'm Peter Taylor," he said. "I'm a reporter for the newspaper *International Times.*" He pulled a notebook out of one of the pockets in his vest. "Tell me more about these cranes."

Nate, Rashel, Mick, and Jessica each took a turn telling part of the story. They told the reporter how there were few wattled cranes left in Africa. They explained the research that Nev was doing to try to save the cranes and how they were helping him. And then they told him about the fire and digging the firebreak.

"If we hadn't stopped the fire," Jessie continued, "it would have swept into Area 2.

The chicks are still too young to fly. They would have died."

Mick nodded. "The crane population can't afford to lose any chicks. They're already at risk from so many other things." He looked over at the two men from the pipeline company. "And building pipelines could put the cranes' habitat at risk, too."

"What do you mean?" the reporter asked.

The two men heard what Mick said. They were both scowling. One looked really angry. "He doesn't mean anything!" he growled. "He's just a child. We've spent enough time here! Let's go right now!"

But Peter didn't seem to want to go. "Hang on a minute," he said. "I've just got a few more questions for these kids."

The interns explained how fragile the cranes' wetland home is. They explained how pipelines carrying water away from the Okavango Delta could destroy the wetlands.

"Taking water from the delta might change it," Rashel said. "Okavango might change so much that the cranes couldn't nest here anymore. Then what would they do?"

Peter shook his head. "I don't know. But this all sounds pretty serious." He asked more questions. He took two more pages of notes. The entire time the two men were getting angrier.

Finally, the blonde man couldn't stand it any more. He pounded his fist on the wing of the airplane. "Taylor! We asked you to come to Okavango to tell our story! Forget the kids!"

The reporter seemed to stiffen. "I think there's another story here," he said. He spoke so softly only Nev and the interns could hear him.

He stepped back. "All done!" he called over his shoulder to the men. "Just a few photographs." He snapped some pictures of Nev and the interns standing with their shovels and buckets.

"Thanks very much for taking the time to talk to me," Peter Taylor said, rather loudly. "You're very brave kids." Then he dropped his voice to barely a whisper. "And you've told me a very interesting story. It's one that I think my newspaper will print."

Then he winked at the interns. He turned and walked back to the plane and climbed in.

Nev and the interns stood and watched the plane take off. It roared up into the sky. They watched as it got smaller and smaller until it was just a tiny dot among the clouds.

Jessie leaned on her shovel and sighed. "Peter was nice. But do you really think he'll print our story?" She turned to look at Nev. He nodded. The corners of his mouth turned up. He smiled. Then he grinned. Then Nev burst out laughing. He laughed until tears ran down his cheeks.

The interns stared at the scientist, wondering if he'd gone crazy.

Finally, Nev stopped laughing. He wiped his eyes. "For two whole years I've been trying to get a reporter to write about how the cranes and the Okavango Delta would be endangered by pipelines. And now you, my young friends, have not only saved many chicks from the fire, but you have also convinced that reporter to tell the cranes' story to the world!"

"We did?" Rashel asked.

Nev nodded. "You most certainly did. I'd guess he'll have the story written and sent off to his paper before the end of the day."

"Cool!" cried Mick. "Maybe Dr. Bender will see the article! He'll learn what we're doing— even before he reads our journals!"

Jessie suddenly looked concerned. "Maybe we should have told Peter more about the cranes. You know, things like how many nests there are, how fast the chicks are growing, how many . . . ."

Nev put a hand on her shoulder. "No, Jessie. You told him just enough. You told him a good story, a story that he will print and thousands of people will read."

Nev reached down and picked up his canteen. He unscrewed the cap. He held the canteen high in the air.

"Ladies and gentlemen," he said proudly, "I would like to make a toast!"

The interns looked at each other. Then they reached for their own canteens and held them up toward Nev.

"To the cranes," Nev said, "and the people who are working to save them! PULA!"

"PULA!" shouted the interns, knocking their canteens together. Then each of them took a long drink of the cool, clear water—the same water that brought life to the Okavango Delta deep in the heart of Africa.